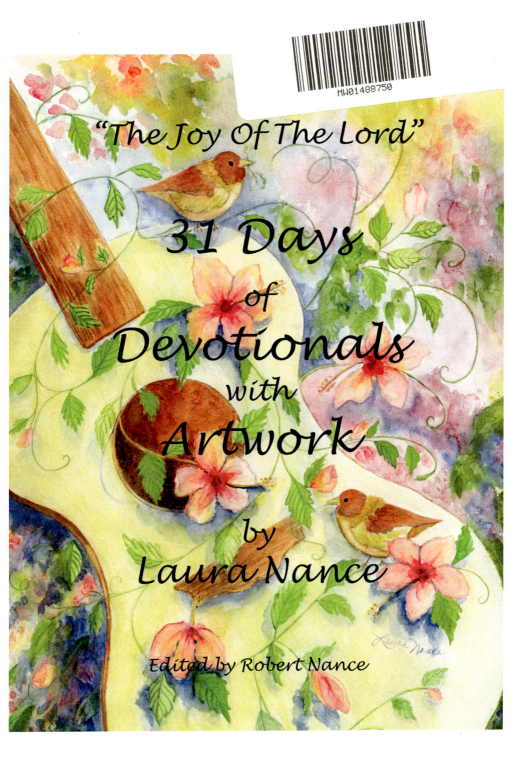

"The Joy Of The Lord"

31 Days

of

Devotionals

with

Artwork

by

Laura Nance

Edited by Robert Nance

"The Joy Of The Lord"

31 Days
of
Devotionals
with
Artwork

by
Laura Nance

Edited by Robert Nance

Table of Contents

Devotionals / Artwork

REJOICE IN THE LORD

"Rejoice in the Lord always; and again I say, Rejoice."
Philippians 4:4

This Scripture in Philippians was penned by a prisoner who for many years had been mobbed by riotous crowds, had suffered brutal beatings and had been stoned by those who sought to destroy him and the Gospel he preached. The Apostle Paul goes on to say in Philippians 4:13 "I can do all things through Christ who strengthens me".

Whether we find ourselves in a situation which is bright as a sunny day or as problematic and dim as darkest night, we are to rejoice. Joy is a fruit of the Spirit. Joy is an awareness of God's supernatural love for us. Joy in the Lord is continuous, based on the relationship we have as His children, while happiness may come and go relative to our circumstances. God's Word commands us to rejoice even during those times when the going gets rough and there are no visible means of support.

"Yet I will rejoice in the LORD, I will joy in the God of my salvation."
Habakkuk 3:18

In Hebrew the word "rejoice" means to jump up and down, and "joy" is to spin around (hilarious, jubilant).

We can weep over circumstances but at the same time we are to be mindful that our mighty and powerful God, who loves us with a true and everlasting love, is faithful and able to supply all of our needs through Jesus Christ our Lord. Rejoice in the Lord... always!

IN THE SHADOW OF HIS WINGS

"On my bed I remember You; I think of You through the watches of the night. Because You are my help, I sing in the shadow of Your wings. I stay close to You; Your right hand upholds me." Psalm 63: 6-8

God cares immeasurably for each one of us. Our all knowing, all powerful God has a plan for our lives. He wants us to call upon Him in good times as well as trying times. God desires that we fellowship with Him. God protects His children, who find refuge under the shadow of His wings.

During a time of fierce pursuit by Saul, David fled to the wilderness of Judah. God gave David Psalm 63 in the midst of this desperate situation, and David cried out to the Lord: *"O God, You are my God, earnestly I seek You, my soul thirsts for You, my body longs for You, in a dry and weary land where there is no water." Psalm 63:1*

David goes on to praise the Lord: *"I will praise You as long as I live, and in Your Name I will lift up my hands." Psalm 63:4*

Whether you find yourself in a desert place or on rich fertile soil would you, like David, take a moment to sing praise to Him as you are resting under the shadow of the infinitely vast protective wings of the Almighty God?

COMMIT YOUR WAY TO THE LORD

"Commit your way to the LORD, trust also in Him, and He shall bring it to pass." Psalm 37:5

Come to God with each decision to be made - even when the step you are about to take seems "obvious" to you. Our finite minds can't comprehend our infinite God's thoughts and ways. We must lean on Him... seek His direction... His will. We are often unwilling to wait... we fail to trust in His timing. Our omniscient God knows what He is doing... He has a plan for my life... a plan for your life!

We need not be fearful and anxious... our God is faithful and just to calm our hearts and strengthen us.

"The steps of a good man are ordered by the LORD, and He delights in his way. Though he fall, he shall not be utterly cast down; for the LORD upholds him with His hand." Psalm 37:23-24

STEADFASTLY ANCHORED

"This hope we have as an anchor of the soul, both sure and steadfast."
Hebrews 6:19a

Having sailed for years on ships, I can still recall the sound of the massive anchors being lowered to secure the ship from the movement of the waves and the ever changing currents. It was always a comforting assurance after a week on stormy seas and a reminder that Jesus is my sure and steadfast hope.

We read in Hebrews 6:18 that we are to lay hold of the hope set before us. As we see the tide of "the world" change, drifting further and further away from the things of God, we need to draw near to Jesus, our anchor of the soul.

If our excitement in living for Christ has faded and we're taking Him for granted, then perhaps Christ in us is no longer real to us. If the Bible is no longer alive to us, prayer no longer vital for us and fellowship has become inconvenient... well, as far as walking in the Spirit... we have become more like spectators of Christ than followers of Christ.

As believers, we have access to God through Jesus Christ. Knowing Jesus lives to intercede for us should change the way we think about ourselves and keep us from going adrift. It bears repeating... we need to lay hold of Jesus, our anchor of the soul.

Return to your First Love! Get into the Word, pray, fellowship, serve the Lord with gladness!

"Blessed is the man who trusts in the LORD, and whose hope the LORD is."
Jeremiah 17:7

HIS PEACE

"Be anxious for nothing, but in everything by prayer and supplication, with thanksgiving, let your requests be made known to God; and the peace of God, which surpasses all understanding, will guard your hearts and minds through Christ Jesus." Philippians 4:6-7

When we truly are "anxious for nothing", pray about everything and give thanks to God for all things, we come to know the awesome blessing of this profound peace which surpasses all measure of our finite understanding.

On a cold winter afternoon, a friend of ours was driving with her two handsome young sons, down a winding mountain road. As she anticipated they might encounter patches of ice along the way, she drove cautiously.

During the usual series of twisting turns, at one of the steepest points of the drive, the car began to slide over the icy roadway. Unable to steer, she said: "boys the car is out of control". In spite of the helpless situation, she found she was experiencing absolute calm and peace.

Suddenly, the car stopped; one of the front wheels was hanging off the side of the mountain. They were astounded to see that the wheel was actually leaning against a very small tree, which was jutting up from below. Yes, from all appearances, they were that close to plunging to the ground thousands of feet below. Yes, the little tree God had planted had blocked their fall. They gave thanks and praise to God.

God knows the number of hairs on our heads; God knows the number of our days. Let us be reminded to keep our communication with God open. When we are in touch with Him on a regular basis - in His Word, in prayer and with thanksgiving - His peace, which surpasses all understanding will guard our hearts and minds through Christ Jesus, no matter what our circumstances.

FAITH IN THE TRUE AND LIVING GOD

"Now faith is the substance of things hoped for, the evidence of things not seen." Hebrews 11:1

We may not always see what God sees but we can believe what God says.

Concerning the choices we make each day, we must choose to draw close to the true and living God and listen for His voice. We must desire His perfect will.

People and circumstances might oppose us but God has a master plan. He can out-play any man or the devil. God is in control; He is superior to all!

When we can't see God working in our lives and we ask "why", or when we think our experience is not matching our expectation it's because we're trusting in our own finite understanding. It is only when we seek God's infinite wisdom that we will not be asking why and we will not be questioning our experience.

"And we know that all things work together for good to those who love God, to those who are the called according to His purpose."
Romans: 8:28

THE POTTER AND THE CLAY

"But now, O LORD, You are our Father. We are the clay, and You our Potter; and all we are the work of Your hand." Isaiah 64:8

We read, in the book of Genesis, that God formed man from the dust of the earth. We were created in His image and we were created for His pleasure!

Every one of us is unique; God didn't use a cookie-cutter when He formed us. We should not be trying to squeeze ourselves into a mold nor should we be interfering with God's work in other people's lives.

A dear woman once shared with us, how years before when she saw herself as more "spiritual" than her husband, she attempted to get him more involved in the things of God. The harder she tried, the less interested he became.

One day, God gave her a vision: A potter was standing at a potter's wheel, patiently and lovingly shaping a clay pot. She then saw how when He left that piece of pottery to work on another, a little hand came up from behind and began to reshape the pot, squishing and patting along the edges.

She realized the "Potter" was the Lord and the clay pot, her husband. Every time God was working in her husband's life and heart, she would come along and mess things up. She repented, stopped interfering, and then marveled at how God worked in and through her husband's life, shaping him into a Godly man.

You may want to take a moment to consider the condition of your own heart. Is it a brittle or splintered piece of pottery? Or is your heart soft and supple clay, ready and eager to be shaped and molded by the hand of the Master Potter?

Our God wants to work in the internal and on the eternal, whereas we often get in the way, working on the external.

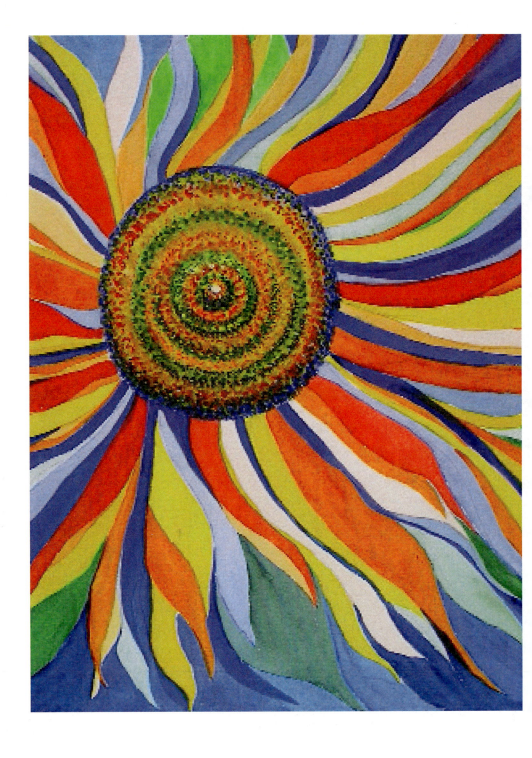

WALK IN TRUTH

Jesus said... *"If you abide in my word, you are my disciples indeed. And you shall know the truth, and the truth shall make you free." John 8:31-32*

We get to know the true and living God as we read and study His Word. The Word of God is our instruction manual. God will work through the Scriptures to separate the spiritual things from the soulish things. The Spirit of God in your heart and mind will allow you to say "no" to the things of darkness. The Truth sets us free from bondage.

"For I rejoiced greatly when brethren came and testified of the truth that is in you, just as you walk in the truth. I have no greater joy than to hear that my children walk in truth." 3 John 1:3-4

I thought about how, as a small child, on one occasion my Mom looked me in the eye and said: "Tell me the truth, just tell me the truth". I was startled. "Wow... Mom is so serious... the truth must be very important", I considered. Little did I realize that one day many years later, something far more startling would happen to me. It was that precious day when through His mercy and grace, I came to know the true and living God and recognize the Truth of His Living Word. How glorious to know that I will spend eternity thanking, praising and worshiping Him... Hallelujah!

The entirety of your word is truth, and every one of your righteous judgments endures forever. Psalm 119:160

ABIDING IN THE VINE

"I am the true vine, and My Father is the vinedresser. Every branch in Me that does not bear fruit He takes away; and every branch that bears fruit He prunes that it may bear more fruit." John 15:1-2

God the Father is the "vinedresser", Jesus is the "true vine" and the Holy Spirit is the "living water". We are the branches of the true vine. Jesus goes on to say, in *John 15:4: "Abide in Me and I in you, as the branch cannot bear fruit of itself, unless it abides in the vine, neither can you, unless you abide in Me".*

We cannot bear fruit unless we abide in Christ. Have you been abiding in Christ? Have you been listening earnestly and longingly for the voice of the LORD God? Have you been seeking Him each day? If so, have you felt the gentle loving touch of the Master Gardener as you walked along the garden path? Have you been reaping the benefits of His love and wisdom so as not to face the challenges of life in your own inadequate strength and ability?

While preparing a study relating to "The Master's Garden", I was typing Eve's response to God (Genesis 3:13). "And the LORD God said to the woman, 'What is this you have done?' And the woman said, 'The serpent deceived me, and I ate." My fingers somehow had moved out of place on the keyboard, and I looked up to see that what I had typed as Eve's response was gibberish. How appropriate - we need to be mindful that when we do anything, outside of the will of God, the results will be unfruitful; and our excuses, merely gibberish.

As we abide in Christ, God cultivates the soil and removes the choking, damaging and entangling weeds so that we can bear abundant fruit. God wants to create a clean fertile heart in each of us. Let us praise God as He does the pruning, as it is He who works everything together for the good for those who are the called according to His purpose. Rejoice! He is preparing you and me for the ultimate harvest.

"Blessed is the man who trusts in the LORD and whose hope is in the LORD. For he shall be like a tree planted by the waters, which spreads out its roots by the river, and will not fear when heat comes, but its leaf will be green, and will not be anxious in the year of drought, nor will cease from yielding fruit." Jeremiah 17:7-8

HIS BURDEN IS LIGHT

"Come to Me, all you who labor and are heavy laden, and I will give you rest. Take My yoke upon you and learn from Me, for I am gentle and lowly in heart, and you will find rest for your souls. For My yoke is easy and My burden is light." Matthew 11:28-30

Come - you who are pressured by the world's standards and demands, which lead to stress and anxiety, and cause you to grow weary and your heart to grow bitter.

Are you carrying a heavy burden you have put on yourself; or, have others placed unreasonable burdens upon you?

We really need to "know" God, as revealed through Jesus, to have peace. Jesus is gentle... humble and sweet. When we take our eyes off Jesus we become anxious and frustrated and we lose the rest we have in Him.

Jesus said "My burden is light". His joy is to please the Father. How awesome. Consider this... it is easier to please the Father than to please man.

Turn your eyes upon Jesus - let go of anxious thoughts and cares and in Him you will find rest, peace and abundant joy - His yoke is easy, His burden is light.

THE LOVE OF GOD

"For I am persuaded that neither death nor life, nor angels nor principalities nor powers, nor things present nor things to come, nor height nor depth, nor any other created thing, shall be able to separate us from the love of God which is in Christ Jesus." Romans 8:38-39

If you are a child of God and you feel under condemnation, it is not of the Lord. To feel unworthy or undeserving is of the enemy. God loves us. In Romans 8:31 we read: "If God be for us, who can be against us?"

An unexpected corporate re-structuring decision was made which was to affect several people... including myself. When it occurred, none of us were able to see God's hand in the change. Feeling wounded, rejected and personally challenged, my immediate thought was: "Lord, is this of You... or is this of man? I feel like a dog".

The following morning, after a time of prayer and Bible study at home, I was walking downstairs and encountered a most delightful and unusual sight. At the front door there were two dogs, each staring in through the window on either side of the door. Wagging their tails, they appeared to be "smiling". How lovingly they gazed at me. I felt overwhelmed with a sense of joy and the love of the Lord.

The animals somehow got loose when neighbors had left their home that morning. I noticed the dogs were not conducting themselves in a disagreeable or sorrowful way - they seemed to have absolute trust that their master would not forsake them. I was reminded that my Master, my loving God had not forsaken me. God tells us in His Word: "I will never leave you nor forsake you".

We can weep over circumstances but at the same time we can rejoice in the Lord. We must keep our eyes on the Lord - He is in control. We need to hold on to the truth of the Word. As long as we are in Christ Jesus, nothing can cause us to be separated from the love of God.

GOD WANTS TO COMPLETE THE WORK IN OUR LIVES

"Being confident of this very thing, that He who has begun a good work in you will perform it until the day of Jesus Christ." Philippians 1:6

We lose hope when we forget who God is. Many people want to throw in the towel when they pray and God doesn't respond in the way they would like Him to... according to their own opinion or plan. They may even begin to question why God doesn't work in a more visible, tangible way.

Our loving God cares for our every need. We must change our minds about how we think God works and place our trust in His power and strength to follow through on whatever He shows us to do. He is faithful to lead us safely on the right path. Let us determine in our hearts to go forth in Christ, in His strength, with steadfastness, stability and service.

God wants to complete the work in our lives.

DON'T LET YOUR GUARD DOWN

"Put on the whole armor of God, that you may be able to stand against the wiles of the devil. For we wrestle not against flesh and blood, but against principalities, against powers, against the rulers of the darkness of this world, against spiritual wickedness in high places." "Wherefore, take unto you the whole armor of God, that you may be able to withstand in the evil day, and having done all to stand." Ephesians 6:11-13

God's Word instructs us to "put on the whole armor of God" - not just part of the armor, the whole armor - the complete covering. Leave no opening through which the enemy can enter. The devil wants to devour and destroy. The enemy sees our nakedness and vulnerability. He knows where we are weak - the battle is fierce. The enemy wants control of our minds. Sometimes there are tests, trials or attacks. When the fiery darts hit - home... relationships... job... finances... health... etc. we need to use the right weapons. Stay dressed in the whole armor of God - don't let your guard down. If you don't understand it is a spiritual battle up front, you are not going to stand!

When fear hits... it is not of God! The mind of the flesh is death. The mind of the spirit is life and peace. Sometimes in our moment of pain, weakness, anxiety... we lose perspective. Trust God.

When we delight in God's Word; when we seek and trust our God of grace and mercy, we can find rest, even while in the midst of a storm, knowing for certain that God is working everything together for our good! "And we know that all things work together for good to those who love God, to those who are the called according to His purpose." Romans 8:28

"Stand therefore, having girded your waist with truth, having put on the breastplate of righteousness, and having shod your feet with the preparation of the gospel of peace, above all, taking the shield of faith with which you will be able to quench all the fiery darts of the wicked one. And take the helmet of salvation, and the sword of the Spirit, which is the word of God; praying always with all prayer and supplication in the Spirit being watchful to this end with all perseverance and supplication for all the saints." Ephesians 6:14-18

FLOWERING IN THE SON

"But the fruit of the Spirit is love, joy, peace, patience, kindness, goodness, faithfulness, gentleness, self-control. Against such there is no law."
Galatians 5:22-23

Sunflowers are particularly neat... as they grow they seem to be reaching with outstretched arms to the heavens above. Their cheerful faces greet the morning sun with a smile, and their uplifted heads follow its path of light throughout the day. Oh, that we would do the same.

We must ask ourselves... Is the Word of God planted in my heart? Am I speaking to God in prayer and listening for and to His voice each day? Am I worshiping Him, praising Him and in fellowship with other believers on a regular basis? Am I bearing the fruit of His Spirit?

"I am the vine, you are the branches. He who abides in Me, and I in him, bears much fruit; for without Me you can do nothing." John 15:5

Let the sunflower be a reminder for us to greet the SON in the morning with a smile and to keep our eyes focused on Him every moment of the day!

May you be mightily blessed as you seek His face and bear abundant fruit!

LIGHT

"For you were once darkness, but now you are light in the Lord. Walk as children of light." Ephesians 5:8

Ephesians 4:30-32 gives insight to what may cause us to walk in darkness rather than light. Importantly, Scripture reveals the remedy for this condition. *"Grieve not the Holy Spirit of God, by whom you are sealed unto the day of redemption. Let all bitterness, and wrath, and anger, and clamor, and evil speaking, be put away from you, with all malice; and be you kind one to another, tenderhearted, forgiving one another, even as God, for Christ's sake has forgiven you."*

If you find yourself venturing out into spiritually dark areas where you can readily plunge downward, think prayerfully and not pridefully about the steps you are taking. It takes "Light", the Holy Spirit, for you to "see". The Spirit reveals the truths of God. When your eyes are open to the Spirit... your whole life is light.

In Matthew's Gospel Jesus tells us that we are "the light of the world". We are to be walking in light.

KEEP AN ETERNAL PERSPECTIVE

"Lay up for yourselves treasures in heaven, where neither moth nor rust destroys and where thieves do not break in and steal. For where your treasure is, there your heart will be also." Matthew 6:20-21

Millions of people in this world are seeking, searching and longing - hoping the realization of some earthly pursuit will fill the deep well of emptiness that gnaws at them from within.

Material "stuff" causes us to be worried and frustrated, whereas the things of the Spirit bring hope and peace. You may be among the many individuals who have suffered extensive loss due to the financial crisis in the world today, but you say you are still hopeful. Is your hope in man and mammon? Or is your hope in God Who created Heaven and earth?

Shortly after becoming a Spirit-filled believer, as I earnestly prayed for cleansing and the humility to totally surrender myself, God showed me something amazing. I suddenly had a clear picture of certain things which needed to be changed or removed from my life. One by one, as these encumbrances were discarded I experienced a sense of freedom and peace beyond what I could ever have imagined.

You can never be satisfied with the "stuff" you collect. Jesus warns us against laying up earthly treasures, which will ultimately prove to be worthless. Whether you invest in earthly treasures or heavenly treasures affects who you are and where your heart is. Do you have something you know God is showing you to surrender to Him today?

We need not waste too much time with temporal things; we need to keep an "eternal perspective".

"Therefore I say to you, do not worry about your life, what you will eat or what you will drink; nor about your body, what you will put on. Is not life more than food and the body more than clothing? Look at the birds of the air, for they neither sow nor reap nor gather into barns; yet your heavenly Father feeds them. Are you not of more value than they?" Matthew 6: 25-26

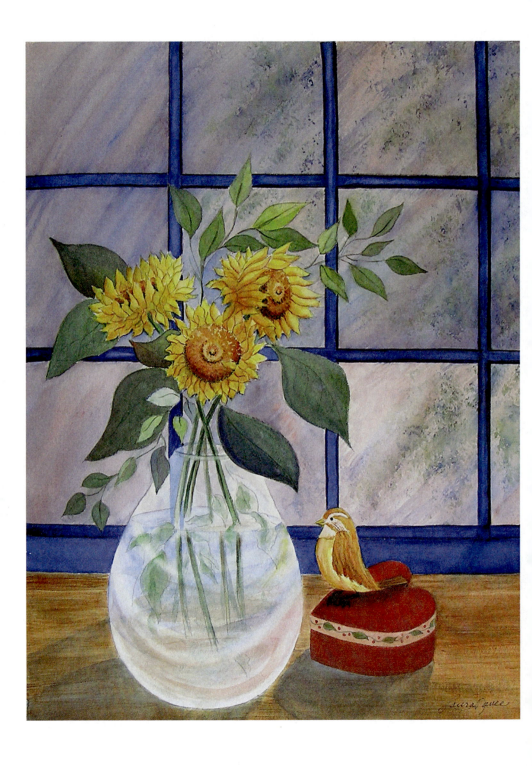

A REFLECTION OF HIS HOLINESS

"God be merciful to us and bless us and cause His face to shine upon us, that Your way may be known on earth, Your salvation among all nations."
Psalm 67:1-2

Our desire should be to reflect the beauty of the Kingdom so we can introduce others to the King. We must allow ourselves to become a reflection of Him.

God is awesome - we will tremble in His presence - the splendor of His holiness is ultimately compelling. People are attracted to the beauty of Jesus and His holiness attracts people. People see His holiness and attractiveness through us when He is reflected in our lives.

"I sought the LORD, and He heard me, and delivered me from all my fears. They looked to Him and were radiant, and their faces were not ashamed. This poor man cried out, and the LORD heard him and saved him out of all his troubles. The angel of the LORD encamps all around those who fear Him and delivers them. Oh taste and see that the LORD is good. Blessed is the man who trusts in Him." Psalm 34:4-8

THE SERVANT I SO LONG TO BE

"...And whatever you do, do it heartily, as to the Lord and not to men, knowing that from the Lord you will receive the reward of the inheritance; for you serve the Lord Christ. But he who does wrong will be repaid for the wrong which he has done, and there is no partiality." Colossians 3:23-25

To be called a servant of God is an honor and a privilege. In no way is it to be considered a menial position. A servant of God is characterized by humility and concern for others, and is moved by a sincere desire to do God's will. We are to be a bondservant (Greek - doulos) of Christ. We are both to serve the Lord as a doulos, and to serve others as a diakonos. (Greek for helper or minister). (Colossians 3:24) Consider these words to the following song:

*"MAKE ME THE SERVANT"

Shield my ears to words of praise which aren't meant for You.
Keep my heart from selfish thoughts; take away all my fleshly desire.

Cradle me in Your arms each day just like a newborn babe,
Lord help me to never go astray, let me walk in the light of Your Word.

Make me the servant I so long to be, break me into Your humble child.
Filled with Your Spirit 'til all shall see… Jesus living in me.

Cover my sight to the lusts of the world; help me to see through Your eyes.
Open my lips to speak boldly of You, Lord teach me to share Your love.

Make me the servant I so long to be, break me into Your humble child.
Filled with Your Spirit 'til all shall see… Jesus living in me…
Jesus living in me.

*Lyrics taken from: "Jesus Only You" CD by Robert and Laura Nance

"If anyone serves Me, let him follow Me; and where I am, there My servant will be also. If anyone serves Me, him My Father will honor." John 12:26

WHAT ABOUT YOU AND ME?

"Humble yourselves, therefore, under the mighty hand of God, that He may exalt you in due time, casting all your care upon Him for He cares for you."
1 Peter 5:6-7

When trials come be humble and submissive - not prideful and angry... God resists the proud... He gives Grace to the humble.

Years ago, in my place of employment, an individual in a supervisory position caused much grief and dismay in the hearts of those of us working there. A couple of my fellow employees literally had nervous breakdowns as a result of the prevailing tone of darkness. The situation was so devastating, I spent a good deal of time pondering over the negative aspects of the predicament and wondering what could be done.

One day while I was praying, I said, "Lord... what are You going to do about that person? How can this keep going on? What can I do about this person?" Suddenly, the Lord spoke to my heart. "What about you and Me?" I said, "No, I am talking about that person and myself, not about You and me, Lord." Again I heard the same message, as clearly as if audible, and tears began to flow. "What about you and Me?" In that moment I realized that my walk with the Lord was being jeopardized... not by someone else... but by myself. I was spending more time thinking about and stressing over what was going on in the workplace situation, and less time in prayer and in the Word.

When we complain about our lot in life we are complaining about God. We need to seek God's will and ask Him to help us focus so that we are accepting in the midst of what He is doing. God is working His eternal purpose in each of our lives. We are not to try to get God to bless our agenda. How does God accomplish His will in our lives when people and circumstances oppose us? He doesn't cause people to do evil things but He can cause some of the things they do to work for our good. God has a master plan. God is in control... superior to all.

Be confident in the Lord, then even during difficult times... you will be mindful that... He cares for you!

UNWAVERING FAITH

"Now faith is the substance of things hoped for, the evidence of things not seen." Hebrews 11:1

Sometimes our "hope" is in what we know and see. We are prone to examine and analyze rather than trust God and step out in faith. The Scriptures tell us in Hebrews 11:6 that "without faith it is impossible to please God". We read further in chapter 11, that Abraham when he was "called" he "obeyed". God's Word tells us to "walk by faith and not by sight". This is what Abraham did.

Money can buy a mountain, but faith can move a mountain. Pray for faith - unwavering faith. While faith does not eliminate problems, when I surrender and yield, God will be in control. Faith will provide an acceptance in my heart of what God is working out in my life; faith will sustain me in the hour of trial.

Are you willing to surrender, to trust God and accept His provision and plan for your life? Is your hope in the Lord who made Heaven and Earth? Do you have unwavering faith and peace with God?

"Therefore, having been justified by faith, we have peace with God through our Lord Jesus Christ, through whom also we have access by faith into this grace in which we stand, and rejoice in hope of the glory of God." Romans 5:1-2

TREASURE FROM THE HEART OF GOD

"My son, if you receive My Words, and treasure My Commands within you so that you incline your ear to wisdom, and apply your heart to understanding, Yes, if you cry out for discernment, and lift up your voice for understanding, If you seek her as silver, and search for her as for hidden treasures; then you will understand the fear of the LORD, and find the knowledge of God. Proverbs 2:1-5

Are you seeking and trusting God and His Word... or in finite trinkets and worldly possessions?   Are you focusing on eternal security in heaven, or temporal earthly comforts?

In the Gospel of Mark, Chapter 10, when the rich young ruler asked Jesus "What shall I do that I may inherit eternal life?" Jesus said, "You know the Commandments," and He expounded on those. The young man responded that he had observed them from his youth.   Jesus, looking at him, and loving him, said, "One thing you lack: Go your way, sell whatever you have and give to the poor and you will have treasure in heaven; and come, take up the cross and follow Me". We are told that the rich young man was sad at this word, and went away grieved, for he had great possessions.

The affluent young man felt the need for something more. However, his heart was tangled up in material things. He was blinded as to the sin in his life and did not understand just how spiritually impoverished he was. Given the choice to make Jesus the highest priority in his life, the young man couldn't let go of his worldly treasure. Jesus wanted him to see that the very thing he wouldn't let go of was what had a hold on his heart.

Is your heart bound by some earthly treasure, of which you will not let go? Jesus wants us to give up whatever holds us back from a full surrender to Him.

JESUS, THE LIGHT OF THE WORLD

"Let your light so shine before men, that they may see your good works and glorify your Father in heaven." Matthew 5:16

We read in Matthew 5 that we are the light of the world and we are to let our light so shine before men that they may see our good works and glorify our Father, who is in heaven. This light that is in us is Christ. We must be a reflection of the Son within us. Some years ago, I shared the Gospel and prayed with my physician in California, and she asked Jesus into her heart. I had verbally witnessed to her, but she indicated to me that she had seen the light of the Lord in my husband's face... (wow)!

Let us bask in the "Sonshine" of His love, as we walk with Jesus, the "Light of the World".

FERVENT PRAYER

"The effectual fervent prayer of a righteous man avails much."
James 5:16

The Greek word translated "prayer" is deesis, which means to bow down. Fervent prayer is when we are continually, earnestly seeking the Lord God with all our heart. We need to pray humbly with a pure heart. Our hearts should be filled with the love of Christ. We need to pray passionately from deep within. Such prayer is powerful and effective and opens the door for God to do wondrous things.

Many times we pray without being in harmony with God's purpose. Our heart needs to be in harmony with God's heart. God is always ready to receive us and listen to us. Every moment of the day we can come into the presence of God through our relationship with Christ.

How awesome that we have a God who desires to guide, control and lead in every area of our lives. He will balance and bless everything beyond what we can imagine.

When you pray, do you yearn for God's will to be done? Give everything to God in prayer and once you are fully surrendered and desire only His perfect will for your life, you will be able to experience His peace which passes all understanding no matter which direction His hand is guiding you. He may walk you through a sunlit garden or steer you through a dimly lit valley or pilot you up to a mountaintop. He wants to hold you close and embrace you in His love every step of the way.

Are you consistent, persistent and committed to praying? Prayer must be the "first" resort and not the "last" resort.

The Word of God instructs us to: *"Pray without ceasing. In everything give thanks, for this is the will of God in Christ Jesus concerning you."*
1 Thessalonians 5:17-18

ACCORDING TO HIS PURPOSE

"We know that all things work together for good to them that love God, to them who are the called according to His purpose." Romans 8:28

God works out all things for our good. This does not mean all that happens to us is good. We live in a fallen world, but God is with us and God is working His will in our lives.

The MC had already introduced the singer who was about to walk onstage. Due to a malfunction, the mechanical curtain separating the bandstand from the stage was not opening. Microphone in hand, the singer opted not to walk onstage from a lighted area stage right. She was determined to make a grand entrance center-stage. Stepping through the darkened bandstand area, she made her way through the narrow curtain opening which led down to the stage. She will never forget the moment when the heel of her shoe hit the edge of the raised platform causing her to lose her balance. In an instant, she fell to the stage below. The spotlight was on her, but not as she had hoped. Instead of a display of grace and professionalism, she was lying flat on the floor and wriggling to get to her feet.

Fortunately, she chose not to dwell on this moment as a negative, humiliating experience. Instead, she praised the Lord and gave God the glory for His divine protection - Hallelujah - no bones were broken! She truly saw God's hand of Grace in what had transpired; and, her humble response opened a door of opportunity to share the Gospel with those who had witnessed the incident.

God will allow trials and tests. In spite of any difficulty we must not forget God's love for us, and remember that He is in control and has a plan which He is working out for our own eternal good ... according to His purpose!

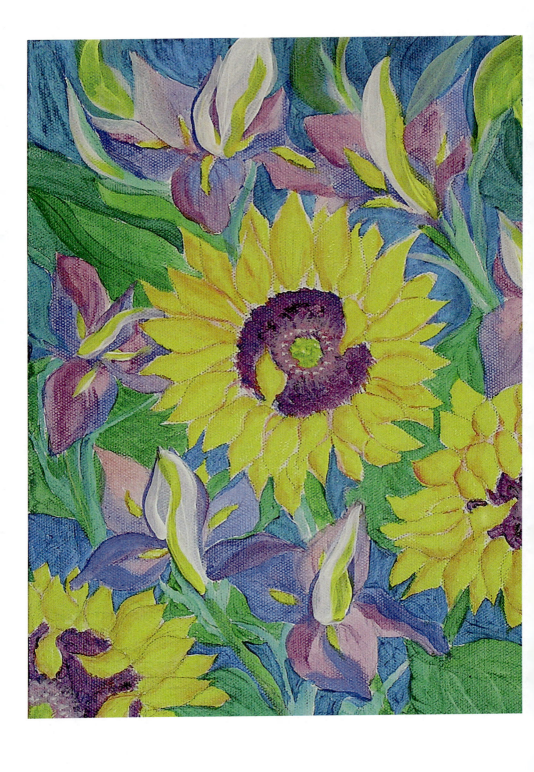

BLOSSOMING AND BEARING FRUIT

"He shall be like a tree planted by the rivers of water that brings forth its fruit in its season, whose leaf also shall not wither; and whatever he does shall prosper." Psalm 1:3

A sign in the produce section of the grocery read: "Meyer Lemons". There was no mistaking the luscious, smooth textured, orange toned beauties which we had never seen displayed in a store until that moment.

I was reminded of the little Meyer lemon tree in our sunroom at home. It blossomed early last spring. Its gorgeous, pungently fragrant flowers then bore tiny beginnings of fruit, which to our disappointment would dry up and drop off.

Oftentimes, we may be blossoming in our walk with the Lord, offering earnest, heart rending prayer as sweet smelling incense to Him. We might possibly begin to serve the Lord but allow the things of this world to divert our attention. We dry up... drop out. We do not bear any fruit.

The word "drop" can be described as falling from a higher place to a lower place. The word "dry" can be defined as thirsty, dehydrated, stale, or parched.

Is God still number one on your list of priorities? Spiritually speaking, have you fallen from a higher place to a lower place? Are you dried up, overcome by the cares of this world? Are you thirsting? Or, are rivers of living water flowing out of your life as the Spirit of God abundantly replenishes you?

The Word of God is overflowing with seeds of promise and hope. God's Word will naturally blossom and bear fruit as it takes root and grows in your heart.

FEARFULLY AND WONDERFULLY MADE

"For You formed my inward parts. You covered me in my mother's womb. I will praise You, for I am fearfully and wonderfully made; Marvelous are Your works, and that my soul knows very well." Psalm 139:14-15a.

Their families were very poor, jobs were hard to come by at the time, but he worked as kitchen help at a restaurant and she at a factory for minimum wage. They got married and rented a small apartment with hopes of furnishing it. Within the first days of marriage the young wife became pregnant. Although hoping one day to have children, they worried that at this moment in their lives they could not afford or provide for a baby. With a remedy recommended by a friend, she attempted to "abort" the baby herself but was unsuccessful. "So we decided to go ahead and have the baby", she said.

Years later, when asked by her daughter... "Mom, why didn't you go to an abortionist"? She answered, "Abortion was illegal at that time and I didn't want to break the law". Wow... can you imagine how bizzare it was for the daughter to learn (according to her Mom), she was born only because abortion was not legal at the time of her conception!?!

How precious it is to know that God's Law never changes... we are each *"fearfully and wonderfully made." Psalm 139:14a "God's eyes saw my substance, being yet unformed in my mother's womb." Psalm 139:16a.* This same child became a Christian and God gave her the blessing of sharing Christ with her mother, who then also gave her life to Christ.

One can't help but ponder how many women opt to abort their babies in this current age as a result of man's law which allows for and encourages abortion. May God be merciful to us all. *"Search me, O God, and know my heart; Try me and know my thoughts; and see if there is any wicked way in me, and lead me in the way everlasting." Psalm 139:23-24*

YOUR HEART

"The heart is deceitful above all things, and desperately wicked; who can know it? I the LORD search the heart, I test the conscience, even to give every man according to his ways and according to the fruit of his doings." Jeremiah 17:9-11

"The Lord sees not as man sees for man looks on the outward appearance, but the Lord looks at the heart." 1 Samuel 16:7

A root of bitterness can grow and make you more and more cynical and disagreeable. We must recognize that God, who searches the innermost depths of our hearts, knows the truth about each one of us.

Praise God, Christian. Our Lord loves us and is a God of grace. He is merciful and ever waiting and wanting to forgive and to cleanse, so that we can start afresh. How great is our God!

LEAN NOT ON YOUR OWN UNDERSTANDING

"Trust in the LORD with all your heart, and lean not on your own understanding." Proverbs 3:5

God will allow trials and tests. In spite of any trial, pain, or rejection... we must never doubt God's love for us... that He is in control and has a plan which He is going to work out for our own good. It is vital that we surrender all to Him and let Him deliver us, heal our wounds and guide us. He will shape us into useful instruments for His purposes.

Are you currently walking in the fullness of the Spirit and able to say, from an eternal perspective, "Yes, Jesus is my Lord and I will do as He says. I trust Him".

Desire to please "self" - leads us to stress and anxiety; it hardens the heart and makes us bitter. When we take our eyes off Jesus we get anxious, we lose our peace, rest and joy.

How are you responding to God with regards to what He is doing in your life today? Let us commit our way unto God. Put our trust in the Lord. God works out all things... not just isolated incidents... for our good.

"In all your ways acknowledge Him, and He shall direct your paths." Proverbs 3:6

OUR SHEPHERD IS ABLE

"All we like sheep have gone astray; we have turned every one to his own way, and the LORD has laid on Him the iniquity of us all." Isaiah 53:6

While brushing our little pup Gabby, I picked several pine needles out of his long hair. He seemed very appreciative.

I started reminiscing about a musician with whom we had worked. While growing up in his native Scotland, he had spent many years as a shepherd. I asked what he considered to be the most difficult problem in caring for sheep. He replied: "Sheep are stupid. If sheep wander into a briar bush, instead of backing away from it, they will push themselves further and deeper until they are so entangled and wounded they will die unless the shepherd comes to their rescue to set them free."

The quickest way for us to get ensnared in bondage is to do what we please rather than what God wants us to do. In Isaiah 53:5 it tells us that Jesus was "wounded for our transgressions, He was bruised for our iniquities".

Are you flirting with or involved in a perilous situation? Are you entangled in a web of helplessness, despair and destruction? God instructs us in His Word, Proverbs 14:12 and 16:25: "There is a way that seems right to a man, but its end is the way of death."

Our Shepherd is able to set us free and apply healing balm to our wounds. *"...I have come that they may have life, and that they may have it more abundantly. I am the Good Shepherd. The Good Shepherd gives His life for the sheep." John 10:10-11*

In *Psalm 23:3* we read: *"He restores my soul; He leads me in the paths of righteousness for His name's sake."* As sheep, we can be stubborn, prideful, indifferent, self-willed. We are prone to wander from the flock, but our faithful Shepherd, filled with loving kindness, will leave the ninety-nine in the flock to rescue me... one stray little lamb. Praise God. Thank you Jesus.

HIS REST

"For he who has entered His rest has himself also ceased from his works as God did from His." Hebrews 4:10

Just as God rested on the seventh day of creation because His work was finished, we can enter into the rest of the finished work of Jesus Christ. Jesus said on the cross "It is finished"! If I truly believe the Good News of the Gospel that Jesus died for my sin... and I am a believer saved by grace through faith, I can trust in the Lord and enter into His rest. Rest is our eternally unshakable relationship with God that can be entered or ignored here on earth as we await the eternal fulfillment to come.

Entering into God's rest is to trust and obey. Not entering into this rest is disobedience. In times of testing and trial we can safely lean on the arm of the "One" who knows what it is to suffer and obey... the "One" who loves us beyond what we can comprehend.

The way we rest and stay in His rest is to give up "trying to make our lives what we want or expect". We need to daily expose ourselves to the Word in a way that allows God to expose the sinful desires of our hearts. The Word of God convicts and corrects as it penetrates into our thoughts. God's Word illuminated by the Spirit can renew us and change us.

Let us strive to rest... pay closer attention to the Word of God... listen to God's voice... trust in God... hold fast to Jesus.

"Let us therefore be diligent to enter that rest, lest anyone fall according to the same example of disobedience. For the Word of God is living and powerful, and sharper than any two-edged sword, piercing even to the division of soul and spirit, and of joints and marrow, and is a discerner of the thoughts and intents of the heart. And there is no creature hidden from His sight, but all things are naked and open to the eyes of Him to whom we must give account." Hebrews 4: 11-13

WALKING HIS WAY

"See that you walk circumspectly, not as fools but as wise. Redeeming the time, because the days are evil. Therefore, be not unwise but understanding what the will of the Lord is." Ephesians 5: 15-17

God's Word reveals that our walk must be careful, diligent, perfect, Spirit-filled. The wise man or woman will seek to know the will of the Lord. It is not wise to lean on my own understanding or leave God out of my plans. God allows us to make choices. As Christians, since we have already chosen His way: repentance, forgiveness, salvation, eternal life... let us delight in walking with the true and living Holy God along the straight and narrow path.

As captives set free, we need not fall prey to entrapments as found in the foolish things of the world. We are victorious in Christ and God does not desire that we miss out on His abundant blessing for us as we follow His perfect plan for our lives. When we delight in the Lord God and hunger and thirst for God's Word... His love-letter to us... we find hope, peace, healing, comfort and joy.

Brothers and sisters in Christ, let us determine, as we awaken each day, to walk His way... circumspectly... as heavenly minded people, who are "heaven bound" for all eternity to come!

Notes

Notes

LAURA NANCE

My desire is to let my paintings reflect the joy and sweetness of a beautiful piece of music. My use of color and light, at times evoking a dreamy world of enchantment and pleasant whimsy, plays in the artwork, as do melody, harmony and rhythm in song. I have an extensive background in the performing arts. I studied and worked as an actress in New York and performed around the world as a professional singer. As an actress it is exciting to dig deep into the soul of the character to be portrayed. As a singer I love getting into the very heart of the lyrics of a song. As a visual artist, I am motivated by the prospect of distilling and applying the "joie de vivre" of a live performance to the visual arts. I'm truly amazed and blessed each time I watch the heart and soul of a painting come to life.

http://laura-nance.fineartamerica.com
www.theartistindex.com/LauraNance/